Fix It In
FOIL

If you're tired of the last-minute scramble to prepare meals – and sick of the clean-up after eating them – foil cookery may be just the answer. With foil, you can prepare food ahead of time, cook it whenever it's convenient and toss away the "pan" when you're done. Foil also keeps food moist and juicy as it locks in flavors and nutrients. So whether you're cooking outside on a grill or campfire or inside in an oven, fix it in foil and enjoy a fabulous meal!

Printed in the United States of America
by G&R Publishing Co.

Distributed By:

507 Industrial Street
Waverly, IA 50677

ISBN-13: 978-1-56383-260-4
ISBN-10: 1-56383-260-7
Item #7024

Table of Contents

Foil Facts & Cooking Tips

Everything you need to know about aluminum foil cooking!

Foil Cooking Basics

Foil can be purchased in two weights: regular or heavy-duty.

Buy and use heavy-duty foil to prevent rips and protect food in high temperatures. If using regular weight foil, use two or three layers.

Foil heats up quickly.

Always use potholders or oven mitts and long tongs to handle foil packs. Support heavy foil packs with a baking sheet when cooking them in an oven or moving the packs to and from a grill or campfire.

Foods wrapped in airtight foil packs will be steamed, not toasted or crunchy.

Choose your foil cooking method by the texture you'd like your food to have after it's cooked. Closed pouches work for foods you wish to steam, like fish and one-dish meals with vegetables. For crisp foods, make and bake them in open foil pans.

You can be burned easily by the steam from a hot foil pack.

The pack becomes a small pressure cooker if it is airtight. To prevent steam burns on your hands or face, carefully open one end of the foil pack first using potholders or oven mitts. This allows some steam to escape from the pack. Then carefully open the top.

Foil makes clean-up easy.

Place hot foil packs on a plate or heat-protected surface. After cutting or unrolling the top of the foil pack, you can eat directly out of the individual packs or transfer food to a serving plate. Throw away the foil after use.

Cooking times will vary. They depend on your heat source, the temperature of the ingredients when you start cooking and the quantity of food you're preparing.

Use the cooking times listed in each recipe as approximate times and check the packs often. Thick foods take longer to cook. Frozen food and foods that have been prepared ahead of time and refrigerated also will require a longer cooking time than foods starting at room temperature.

Oven Basics

Foil can handle hot temperatures.

Foil packs can be baked in the oven at temperatures up to 450°.
If you are simply warming up pre-cooked foods in the oven, use
lower temperatures.

Foil packs can be heavy.

Place foil packs on a baking sheet or shallow pan before putting them
into the oven. Multiple individual packs will fit on one baking sheet, but
allow some space between them. Also, if the foil tears, the baking sheet
catches spills.

Foods cooked in foil packs will not brown like traditional baking.

Use sauces, seasonings and colorful vegetables to make the food
more attractive. Use an accurate food thermometer to check the
internal temperature of meat to determine doneness rather than
relying on appearances.

 When displayed, this icon indicates cooking instructions
for the oven.

Campfire Basics

Foil cooking works best on a two-inch bed of hot coals.

Use charcoal briquettes and/or a wood fire with logs placed in a square, log cabin style, around an A-frame or teepee of tinder in the center. As these fires burn down, the coals will be perfect for foil cooking.

Speed of cooking depends on the temperature of the campfire and what type of food is being cooked.

If coals are too hot, move them apart so food rests on fewer coals, then turn the packs often. You may also place food beside the coals, propping up the packs with rocks. A grill or grate placed above the hot coals at different heights can help fine-tune a campfire's temperature, too.

There's no temperature gauge on a campfire.

Adults can use a "hand thermometer" to check the temperature of the fire and adjust the height of the grill. Carefully hold your hand above the coals (but not above any flames). Move your hand higher or lower to find the temperature you want to use and place your grill there before starting to cook. A simple guideline follows:

- The temperature is about 300° (low heat or warm embers) if you can hold your hand there for four to five seconds.
- The temperature is about 350° (medium heat, coals or embers) if you can hold your hand there for three to four seconds.
- The temperature is about 400° or higher (high heat or hot coals) if it seems very hot and you can hold your hand there for less than three seconds.

Campfire Terms

Coals: In a campfire or charcoal grill, the wood or fuel you cook on after the flames die down.

Embers: Glowing pieces of wood or charcoal briquettes in a campfire or charcoal grill.

 When displayed, this icon indicates cooking instructions for campfires.

Grill Basics

Some foods cook best over direct heat.

For these foods, place foil packs directly over the heat source and cover the grill for even cooking. Rotate or turn packs occasionally during cooking. Carefully open the top of the pack and check food several times to prevent overcooking.

Some foods cook best over indirect heat.

Heat one side of the grill and place these foil-wrapped foods on the other side of the grill so food isn't directly over the heat source. Rotate packs during cooking and cover the grill for even heating.

Charcoal grill temperatures can be adjusted by the quantity of briquettes used.

To reduce the heat, use fewer briquettes, move them around or place them in a single layer. To increase the heat, use more briquettes. Add briquettes around the edges of burning coals to extend the life of the heat when foods require a longer cooking time.

All of these recipes will work on either gas or charcoal grills.

 When displayed, this icon indicates cooking instructions for outdoor charcoal or gas grills.

Foil Packs

Food cooks inside a foil pack by steaming, so the edges of the pack must be sealed well to make it airtight. These packs can be turned over during cooking. An efficient foil pack can be made using a method called the "drugstore wrap." It can be folded flat or tent-style.

How to make a Flat Pack:

This wrap is best for cooking meat, fish and foods that need less steam and more browning.

1. Cut one piece of heavy-duty aluminum foil about twice the distance around the food to be wrapped. It must be long enough to wrap around the food and fold the top and side edges over several times. Don't scrimp on the amount of foil used for each pack.

2. Set the food in the middle of the foil.

3. Bring opposite sides of the foil together above the food and fold them over several times, making a 1″ crease at the top. Fold until foil is flat against the food and top of pack is sealed well.

4. Flatten the ends of the foil pack and fold or roll them together toward the center to make tight seals.

How to make a Tent Pack:

This wrap is best for cooking vegetables, fruits and combination packs that need more steam and less browning.

1. Cut one piece of heavy-duty aluminum foil about twice the distance around the food to be wrapped. It must be long enough to wrap around the food and fold the top and side edges over several times. Don't scrimp on the amount of foil used for each pack.

2. Set the food in the middle of the foil.

3. Bring opposite sides of the foil together above the food and fold them over once to make a 1″ crease at the top. Fold the foil over 2 more times, but leave several inches of space between the food and top of the foil pack, like a tent.

4. Fold or roll the ends of the pack together toward the center to make tight seals.

Tip: Steaming requires moisture from vegetables, water, sauces or ice. Adding two ice cubes to a pack is an easy way to add more moisture.

How to make a 2-Handled Pack:

This wrap allows you to bury the foil pack in coals but have two visible handles to grasp as you remove it from the fire. Since the handles will be hot, use tongs or hot pads.

1. Start by making a flat or tent pack, sealing the long edges together first.

2. Twist the ends of the foil pack like two corkscrews and bend them up to make two handles.

Tip: Even though one layer of heavy-duty foil is adequate for most foil packs, using a double layer is ideal, especially if wrapping large pieces of meat or cooking directly in a campfire. This prevents accidental punctures and also keeps dirt or ashes from touching your food. When you remove the outer layer of foil, the inside package is clean and can be used as the serving dish or plate.

How to make other Foil Cookware:

• **Baking Pan:** Make an open baking pan for foods that need to be crisp or baked. Use a double layer of heavy-duty foil and mold it over an upside-down pan of your choice. Leave extra length at all edges, fold them over and crimp well for strength.

• **Griddle:** Make a griddle for sautéing or frying foods over a campfire by covering a wire rack, grate or grill with a double layer of heavy-duty foil.

FAQs
Frequently Asked Questions About Foil Cooking

How do I prevent over-cooking in a foil pack?
- After making the pack, wrap it in two to three layers of newspaper, then wrap it in another foil pack.
- Surround meats with high-water foods such as slices of onion, tomatoes or cabbage leaves.
- Be diligent about turning your foil packs over or moving them around in the coals so one spot doesn't get too hot.
- Check your packs often during cooking. Carefully open the pack and use a meat thermometer to check the internal temperature of meats. You may also use a fork to check the tenderness of vegetables.

How long should I cook foods?
The recipes in this book give time guidelines, but actual cooking time depends on the size of your foil pack, the reliability of your heat source and the temperature and quantity of food inside each pack. Check your packs often and reseal packs completely before replacing them on the heat. A simple rule of thumb: In combination packs, allow enough time for the slowest food item to cook completely.

How do I know when the meat is fully cooked and safe to eat?
Ground meat, chicken and pork should be cooked until it is no longer pink and juices run clear. But color isn't a fool-proof guide. It is best to use a good meat thermometer to prevent under- or over-cooking. The USDA has these recommendations for minimum internal temperatures:
- Fish: 145°
- Beef Roasts: 145° (rare) to 160° (medium) to 170° (well-done)
- Ground Beef: 160°
- Ground Poultry: 165°
- Chicken Breasts: 170°
- Whole Poultry & Parts (thighs, wings): 180°
- Pork (chops, tenderloins): 160°
- Ground Pork: 160°
- Egg Dishes: 160°
- Reheating Foods: 165° or until hot and steaming

What is the difference between the shiny and dull sides of foil?

Although foil has a shiny and dull side, there actually isn't a great difference in the way they conduct heat and cold. However, for the most efficient use, some general guidelines are:

- To cook in foil, wrap foods with the dull side out so less heat is reflected away and more heat is absorbed.
- To keep foods warm, wrap them with the dull side out.
- To freeze foods, wrap them with the shiny side out.

What is the best type of wood to use in a campfire?

Start the fire with small dry pine branches (kindling) that burn easily. Then switch to hardwood, like the split wood you find at campgrounds. It burns longer and will burn down to make hot coals that provide even heat for cooking. Charcoal briquettes offer another good choice for cooking. After 30 minutes, the briquettes will be covered in gray ash and ready for cooking.

What are some foil No-Nos?

- Do not use foil to cook or store salty, highly-acidic or spicy foods for a long time. The aluminum breaks down and may leave pits in the foil. These won't hurt you, but the pits may cause foil packs to leak.
- Never use foil for microwave cooking. The metal in the foil may cause sparks and arcing.
- Do not use foil to line the bottom of an oven. Instead, cover a baking sheet with foil and place it under the foil pack(s).

Safety Tips

Foil gets hot! Always use potholders or oven mitts to protect your hands. Use long tongs or turners to remove packs from the fire. To avoid steam burns, slowly unwrap cooked packs, starting at the sides.

Fires can be dangerous. Use caution in all cooking and eating activities near campfires and grills. Read the directions for your own equipment and always follow recommended safety procedures and guidelines.

Breakfasts

Great meals to start your day!

Breakfast Cooking Tips

- *For easy camp cooking, mix ingredients ahead of time and store them in zippered plastic bags. Keep the ingredients cold until ready to cook.*

- *Potatoes can be boiled, cooled, sliced and refrigerated ahead of time to be used in foil packs later. This shortens preparation and cooking time.*

- *Spray heavy-duty foil with nonstick vegetable spray or use nonstick foil when cooking eggs, potatoes or starchy foods.*

- *Breakfasts are easy one-dish meals to prepare in advance. Assemble or pre-cook the foods, wrap them in foil and just reheat the foil packs when you are in a time crunch.*

- *Orange shell dishes are best if prepared and assembled just before cooking.*

Foil Pack
Sausage Breakfast

Makes 4 servings

1 lb. ground pork sausage
4 eggs
4 C. frozen, diced hash brown potatoes
Seasoned salt
Salt and pepper

Directions

Divide sausage into 4 equal portions. Flatten each portion into a patty, about ¾″ thick. In a medium bowl, place eggs and scramble well with a fork. Cut heavy-duty foil into 4 (15″) lengths. Spray foil pieces with nonstick vegetable spray. Crimp foil edges enough to prevent spills. Divide hash brown potatoes into 4 equal portions. In the center of each piece of foil, place a portion of the potatoes. Pour about ¼ of the beaten eggs over the potatoes in each pack. Set a sausage patty on top and sprinkle with seasoned salt, salt and pepper to taste. Wrap foil around food in a tent pack.

Cooking Methods

 Preheat oven to 400°. Place foil packs on a baking sheet and bake for 35 to 45 minutes or until sausage and eggs are fully cooked.

 Place double-wrapped foil packs on medium coals and cook for 15 to 25 minutes or until sausage and eggs are fully cooked. Move pack every 5 minutes and turn it over for the last 5 minutes.

 Preheat grill to medium-high heat. Place foil packs on the grill over direct heat, close lid and cook for 20 to 30 minutes or until sausage and eggs are fully cooked. Move pack as needed and turn it over for the last 5 minutes.

Variations

• Use fresh potatoes in place of frozen hash browns. Wash potatoes and cut them into small pieces.

• Sprinkle 2 tablespoons of fresh minced onion and chopped green pepper over the potatoes in each pack before sealing.

• Add sliced green onions, sliced mushrooms and garlic powder to each pack.

• After cooking, open foil pack and place 1 slice of American cheese on top of potatoes in each pack. Let cheese melt before serving.

Western Tortillas

Makes 4 servings

4 eggs
1 C. diced ham
¼ C. chopped green bell pepper
¼ C. minced onions
Salt and pepper
2 tsp. butter, optional
4 flour tortillas
4 slices American cheese
Ketchup, optional

Directions

In a medium bowl, use a fork to scramble eggs with 2 tablespoons water. Add the diced ham, green pepper and onion; mix well. Season with salt and pepper. Cut heavy-duty foil into 2 (12″) lengths. Spray both foil pieces with nonstick vegetable spray. Crimp foil edges enough to prevent spills. Pour half of the egg mixture on the center of each foil piece. If desired, place small pieces of butter on top. Wrap foil around egg mixture in a tent pack.

Wrap tortillas flat in a separate piece of foil. After cooking as directed, open all the foil packs and place 1 slice of American cheese on each warm tortilla. Spoon equal portions of the cooked egg mixture on each warmed tortilla and fold in half or wrap burrito-style to eat. Serve with ketchup, if desired.

Cooking Methods

 Preheat oven to 375°. Place egg foil packs on a baking sheet and bake for 15 to 20 minutes or until eggs are cooked. Warm foil-wrapped tortillas in the oven until soft and pliable. (To warm tortillas in a microwave, wrap tortillas in paper towels instead of foil.)

 Wrap the egg packs in a second layer of foil. Place these foil packs on medium coals for 10 to 15 minutes or until eggs are cooked. Open packs, stir once, and continue to cook if needed. Warm foil-wrapped tortillas on a grill or next to the fire until soft and pliable.

 Preheat grill to medium heat and place egg foil packs on the grill over indirect heat. Close lid and cook for 15 to 20 minutes or until eggs are cooked. Warm foil-wrapped tortillas over indirect heat until soft and pliable.

Variations

• Try other types of cheese, such as Monterey Jack, Cheddar or cream cheese.

• Add bacon bits to the mixture.

• Other vegetables to try are mushrooms and/or diced tomatoes.

• Spice up a plain egg and cheese tortilla with salsa or hot sauce.

• Do-ahead tip: You may scramble the egg mixture in a skillet on the stove, fill the tortillas, fold them burrito style, wrap each one in foil and refrigerate. When it's time to prepare breakfast, just place foil packs in the oven, in hot coals or on the grill until heated through.

Ham and Hash Brown Breakfast

Makes 1 serving

1 C. frozen, shredded hash brown potatoes
¼ C. diced ham
1 T. diced green bell pepper
1 egg
½ tsp. onion powder
Salt and pepper
1 slice American cheese

Directions

In a medium bowl, mix hash browns, diced ham, green pepper, egg, 1 tablespoon water, onion powder, salt and pepper. Cut 1 piece of heavy-duty foil 14″ long. Spray with nonstick vegetable spray. Crimp foil edges enough to prevent spills. Pour egg and potato mixture on foil and seal it tightly in a tent pack.

Cooking Methods

 Preheat oven to 375°. Place foil pack on a baking sheet and bake for 15 to 20 minutes or until egg is cooked through. Carefully open foil pack, place the slice of cheese on top and let it melt before serving.

 Place double-wrapped foil pack on medium coals and cook for 8 to 14 minutes or until egg is cooked but not brown. Turn several times during cooking.

 Preheat grill to medium heat. Place foil pack on the grill over direct heat, close lid and cook for 15 to 20 minutes or until egg is cooked through.

Variations

• Use 1 to 2 tablespoons fresh chopped onion in place of onion powder.

• Add a dash of curry powder for a spicy flavor.

• To prepare 4 servings, cut open a medium bag of shredded hash browns and add the other ingredients directly into the potato bag. Knead bag with hands to mix well, then divide into 4 portions.

• Omit the cheese. Use 2 eggs and 1 slice of bread, torn into small pieces. Mix bread pieces into egg mixture. Dot with small pieces of butter before sealing foil pack.

• Add pieces of cooked bacon, some drained white corn and a few chopped pimientos for a hearty breakfast.

Corned Beef Breakfast Sandwiches

Makes 8 servings

4 English muffins
1 (15 oz.) can corned beef hash
4 green onions, diced
4 slices provolone cheese, cut in half, optional
⅔ C. sour cream
1½ tsp. prepared horseradish
Paprika
Ketchup, optional

Directions

Split the muffins in half and toast them lightly with a toaster or on a piece of foil over a campfire or grill. Spread an equal portion of corned beef hash on each muffin half. Sprinkle some diced green onions over the corned beef. Press down lightly to hold onions in place. Top each one with 1 slice of provolone cheese. In a small bowl, combine the sour cream and horseradish. Spoon an equal portion of this mixture on top of each muffin half. Sprinkle with paprika. Stack 2 (15˝) pieces of heavy-duty foil, shiny side up, and crimp the edges to make an open "tray". Place the open-face muffins on the shiny side of the foil tray. Cook as directed. Serve with ketchup, if desired.

Cooking Methods

 Preheat oven to 400°. Set foil tray on a baking sheet and bake muffins for 10 to 13 minutes or until cheese melts and muffins are heated through.

 Place a grill on top of hot coals. Set foil tray on the grill directly over coals and cook for 8 to 12 minutes or until cheese melts and muffins are heated through.

 Preheat grill to medium-high heat. Set foil tray on the grill over direct heat, close lid and cook for 8 to 12 minutes or until cheese melts and muffins are heated through.

Variations

• Use plain corned beef in place of corned beef hash and omit the cheese.

• Try other types of cheese, such as Cheddar, American or Swiss.

Eggs in an Orange Shell

Makes 2 servings

1 thick-skinned orange
2 eggs
Salt and pepper

Directions

Roll the orange on a hard surface to soften the membranes
inside. Cut the orange in half. Use a sharp knife to separate
the pulp from the white membrane of the shell. With a spoon,
carefully remove all the orange pulp without tearing the peel,
and set fruit aside in a bowl. Crack 1 egg into each hollowed
orange shell. Cut 1 piece of heavy-duty foil for each orange
half. Set each orange half on the foil, keeping the open end
of the orange upright. Wrap foil around oranges in a tent
pack. Flatten bottom of foil so oranges stand upright. Cook
as directed, then season with salt and pepper. Eat the orange
pulp with a spoon or cut it into pieces and combine with other
fruits to make a salad. Eat the cooked egg with the fruit and a
muffin for a complete meal.

Cooking Methods

Preheat oven to 400°. Place foil-wrapped orange halves in a pie tin and bake on the center rack for 10 to 15 minutes or until eggs are fully cooked.

Place foil-wrapped orange halves near hot coals and cook for 5 to 15 minutes or until eggs are fully cooked. Rotate oranges as needed for even cooking, always keeping them upright.

Preheat grill to medium-high heat. Place foil-wrapped orange halves on the grill over direct heat, close lid and cook for 5 to 15 minutes or until eggs are fully cooked.

Variations

• Scramble the eggs with ¼ cup milk before dividing and pouring them into the empty orange shells. Carefully open foil and stir once or twice during cooking time.

• Before serving, sprinkle some shredded Cheddar cheese and cooked bacon bits over cooked eggs.

Muffins in an Orange Shell

Makes 6 servings

6 thick-skinned oranges
1 (7 oz.) pkg. muffin mix, any flavor
Eggs and/or water as directed on muffin mix

Directions

Roll each orange on a hard surface to soften the membranes
inside. Cut off the top fourth of each orange. Use a sharp
knife to separate the pulp from the white membrane of each
shell. With a spoon, carefully remove all the orange pulp
without tearing the peel. Set fruit aside in a bowl to eat later.
Prepare the muffin mix as directed on package. Spoon some
muffin batter into each hollowed orange shell, filling each
about ⅔ full. Cut a 10″ piece of heavy-duty foil for each
orange shell. Set 1 orange on each piece of foil. Wrap foil up
and around sides of shell, flattening bottom and crimping foil
around the top of shell, but leaving the top open. These are
very hot after cooking! Let them cool before eating with a
fork or spoon.

Cooking Methods

 Preheat oven to 400°. Place foil-wrapped orange shells on a baking sheet on the center rack and bake for 25 to 32 minutes or until a toothpick inserted in muffins comes out clean.

 Place foil-wrapped orange shells on hot coals and cook for 10 to 20 minutes. Rotate them as needed for even cooking, always keeping the oranges upright. Remove from coals when a toothpick inserted in muffins comes out clean.

 Preheat grill to medium heat. Place foil-wrapped orange shells on the grill over direct heat, close lid and cook for 15 to 25 minutes or until toothpick inserted in muffins comes out clean. Move to indirect heat if muffins cook too fast

Variations

• Try different flavors of muffin mixes such as blueberry, chocolate, banana, raspberry or lemon poppy seed.

• Stir chopped nuts into the batter.

FYI – The recipes cooked in orange peels may not save any time, but they're fun to do and easy to clean up if you're camping!

27

Spam Squares

Makes 4 to 6 servings

1 (7 oz.) can Spam
4 to 6 slices processed cheese, like Velveeta
¼ C. butter
¼ C. brown sugar
4 to 6 toasted English muffins, optional

Directions

Cut Spam into 6 even slices or 1 slice per person. Cut 1 (10˝) piece of heavy-duty foil for each serving. Place 1 slice of Spam on each piece of foil. Set 1 slice of cheese on top, followed by a sprinkling of brown sugar and a spoonful of butter. Wrap foil around each serving in a flat pack. After cooking as directed, open packs and serve. If desired, place 1 slice of cooked Spam between toasted English muffin halves.

Cooking Methods

Preheat oven to 400°. Place foil packs on a baking sheet and bake for 10 to 15 minutes or until Spam is heated through and cheese is melted.

Place double-wrapped foil packs on hot coals and cook for 5 to 10 minutes or until Spam is heated through. Move packs often to keep heat even.

Preheat grill to medium-high heat. Place foil packs on the grill over direct heat, close lid and cook for 5 to 10 minutes, rotating once, until Spam is heated through.

Variations

• Omit the cheese and replace with a ring of pineapple or candied apple.

• Omit the butter and brown sugar and serve with flavored mustard of your choice.

Main Dishes

Tasty and balanced meals in foil!

Main Dish Cooking Tips

- *Wrap food with a second layer of foil anytime you plan to eat directly from the foil pack.*

- *If you plan to bury foil packs in coals, wrap foil around meal in a 2-handled pack. Allow handles to stick up above coals so you can remove pack easily.*

- *Use colorful vegetables and condiments in foil packs to make meat and seafood dishes more attractive.*

- *To boost the flavor of beef or chicken in foil dinners, add a little beef or chicken bouillon with a very small amount of water.*

- *You can make your own onion soup mix by combining ¼ cup dried minced onion, 2 tablespoons instant beef bouillon and ½ teaspoon onion powder.*

- *After cooking, let meat stand for 10 to 15 minutes before slicing. The internal temperature will continue to increase after meat is removed from heat.*

- *Place a grill or grate over a campfire to cook foods at lower temperatures. The further it is from the fire, the lower the cooking temperature will be.*

- *Chicken breasts larger than 4 ounces must be cooked longer. Always cook poultry until centers are no longer pink and juices run clear (170° inside). Check partway through cooking.*

- *Prepare individual meals in foil packs ahead of time, then refrigerate and cook them as needed. This is a great way for families with busy schedules to eat a nutritious meal anytime.*

- *Hamburger patties can be shaped, wrapped and refrigerated at home, then packed in a cooler to take on a campout.*

31

Basic Beef Hobo Dinner in a Pouch

Makes 4 servings

1 medium onion, peeled and sliced
1 lb. lean ground beef
4 medium potatoes, peeled and sliced
4 medium carrots, peeled and sliced
Salt and pepper
Garlic salt
Seasoned salt
Butter, optional

Directions

Cut 4 (12˝) pieces of heavy-duty foil. Place equal portions of onion slices on each piece of foil. In a medium bowl, combine ¼ cup water and ground beef; mix well. Shape 4 hamburger patties. Set 1 hamburger patty on top of the onions on each piece of foil. Arrange potato and carrot slices on top of each patty. Season with salt, pepper, garlic salt and seasoned salt to taste. Dot with butter if desired. Wrap foil in a tent pack around each serving.

Cooking Methods

 Preheat oven to 350°. Place foil packs on a baking sheet. Bake for 20 to 30 minutes or until vegetables are tender and meat is fully cooked.

 Place double-wrapped foil packs on medium-hot coals for 16 to 25 minutes or until vegetables are tender and meat is fully cooked. Move packs and turn them over once during cooking.

 Preheat grill to medium-high heat. Place foil packs on the grill over direct heat, close lid and cook for 18 to 25 minutes or until vegetables are tender and meat is fully cooked.

Variations

• Substitute 1 bag of mixed frozen vegetables or 1 can of your favorite (drained) vegetable for the fresh potatoes and carrots. Place a few pats of butter on top before sealing foil pouch.

• For a flavorful kick, sprinkle Creole spices or chili powder on meat before adding vegetables.

• Season the ground beef patties with steak sauce, barbeque sauce, Worcestershire sauce, cream of mushroom soup or Italian dressing before cooking.

• Before assembling the foil packs, place 1 cabbage leaf on each piece of foil. Omit water in ground beef. Set foods on the leaf and place a second cabbage leaf on top before wrapping the food in foil. Cabbage leaves add extra moisture, but may be discarded before serving the meal.

• Substitute ground turkey for the ground beef.

Beef Stew

Makes 4 servings

1 lb. beef stew meat
4 slices bacon
4 medium tomatoes
1 C. chopped onions
Beef bouillon granules
Seasoned salt
Salt and pepper
Meat tenderizer, optional
2 potatoes, cubed, optional
2 carrots, sliced, optional

Directions

Cut beef into ¾″ pieces. Cut bacon slices into small pieces. Cut each tomato into quarters. Cut 4 pieces of heavy-duty foil large enough for 1 portion of meat and vegetables. On each piece of foil, place 1 portion of the chopped onions and ¼ pound of beef on top. Sprinkle with bouillon granules, seasoned salt, salt, pepper and meat tenderizer. Arrange bacon pieces and 4 tomato chunks on top of meat in each pack. Add potato cubes and carrot slices to each pack as desired. Wrap foil in a tent pack around each serving.

Cooking Methods

 Preheat oven to 350°. Place foil packs on a baking sheet and bake for 50 to 60 minutes or until meat is fully cooked and tender.

 Wrap the packs in another sheet of foil, making a 2-handled pack with the second layer. Bury the foil packs in warm coals and cook for 40 to 50 minutes or until fully cooked and tender.

 Preheat grill to medium heat. Place foil packs on the grill over indirect heat, close lid and cook for 35 to 45 minutes or until meat is fully cooked and tender.

Variations

• To add more moisture and flavor, add a little butter and 1 tablespoon water, Worcestershire sauce or soy sauce before sealing the foil pack.

• Substitute 1 bag of frozen stew vegetables for the fresh vegetables and use an envelope of stew seasoning plus 4 tablespoons of butter to flavor the packs. Omit the bacon.

• Place all ingredients into 1 single large foil pack. For a different flavor, start with only the stew meat on a large piece of foil. In a medium bowl, combine 1 (2 ounce) package dry onion soup, ½ cup dry red wine or water and ½ envelope Italian salad dressing mix. Add 1 (9 ounce) package frozen mixed vegetables and stir. Spoon mixture over the stew meat in the foil, then wrap the foil pack and cook for about 60 minutes. If desired, stir in ½ cup sour cream just before serving.

Yummy Meatloaf
Makes 6 to 8 servings

2 lbs. lean ground beef
1 egg
½ C. seasoned bread crumbs
Salt and pepper
½ (10 oz.) can tomato soup
Ketchup, optional

Directions
Cut 2 pieces of heavy-duty foil large enough to wrap around
the ground beef. Place the ground beef in the center of 1 piece
of foil and make a large well in the middle of the meat. Crack
the egg into the well. Add the bread crumbs, salt, pepper and
tomato soup. Mix the ingredients together with your hands
until well-blended. Shape loaf as desired but not too thick.
Wrap foil in a flat pack around the loaf. Turn pack over and
wrap it in a second layer of foil, again in a flat pack. Cook as
directed. Before serving, top with ketchup.

Cooking Methods

 Preheat oven to 350°. Place foil pack on a baking sheet and bake for 50 to 60 minutes or until meat is fully cooked.

 Place foil pack on medium embers and cook for 30 to 40 minutes or until loaf is cooked through. Turn pack over several times during cooking and move as needed to obtain even heating.

 Preheat grill to medium heat. Place foil pack on the grill over direct heat, close lid and cook for 30 to 40 minutes or until meat is fully cooked. Turn pack over several times during cooking to obtain even heating.

Variations

- Divide mixture into individual portions and wrap separately in foil. Cut cooking time to about 15 to 25 minutes or until meat is fully cooked.

- For Italian Meat Loaf, omit bread crumbs and tomato soup. Use ½ cup long grain rice, 1 (6 ounce) can tomato paste, 2 tablespoons water and a 1 (2 ounce) package spaghetti sauce mix. Mix well and cook as directed.

- Instead of topping the cooked meatloaf with plain ketchup, in a small bowl mix ¼ cup ketchup, 2 teaspoons Worcestershire sauce and 1 to 2 teaspoons yellow mustard. Combine and spread over cooked meatloaf before serving.

Hobo Chicken Breasts

Makes 4 servings

1 onion, thinly sliced
2 medium potatoes, thinly sliced
2 medium carrots, thinly sliced
3 T. butter or margarine
4 boneless, skinless chicken breast halves
1 (8 oz.) can whole kernel corn, drained
½ tsp. dried thyme
½ tsp. dried rosemary
1 tsp. salt
¼ tsp. pepper

Directions

Spray 1 (18˝) square of heavy-duty foil with nonstick vegetable spray. Arrange the sliced onions in the center of foil. Set the sliced potatoes and carrots on top of the onions. Scatter pieces of butter over vegetables. Arrange chicken breast halves on top of vegetables, overlapping edges as needed. Pour drained corn on and around chicken. Sprinkle thyme, rosemary, salt and pepper on top. Wrap foil in a tent pack.

Cooking Methods

 Preheat oven to 400°. Place the foil pack on a baking sheet and bake for 40 to 50 minutes or until chicken and vegetables are fully cooked.

 Place double-wrapped foil pack on medium embers and cook for 30 to 40 minutes or until chicken and vegetables are fully cooked Move pack and turn it over several times for even cooking. Check after 20 minutes.

 Preheat grill to medium-high heat. Place foil pack on the grill over indirect heat, close lid and cook for 30 to 40 minutes or until chicken and vegetables are fully cooked.

Variations

• To make individual packs, combine desired vegetables and seasonings with each chicken breast half and wrap separately in a smaller piece of foil. Cook single packs for 15 to 30 minutes or until chicken is fully cooked.

• To make Lemon Chicken, brush chicken breast halves with melted butter. Squeeze juice from 1 lemon over the pieces. Sprinkle with salt and lemon pepper but omit the other seasonings. Wrap and cook chicken breasts with the vegetables as directed.

• Make individual Hawaiian Chicken packs by coating each plain chicken breast half with teriyaki sauce or marinade. Place each coated chicken breast half on a piece of foil. Top with slices of green and red bell pepper, chopped onion and pineapple chunks. Wrap foil around food in tent packs and cook for 15 to 30 minutes or until chicken is fully cooked. Serve over rice.

Pizza Chicken

Makes 4 servings

4 boneless, skinless chicken breast halves
1 C. pizza sauce
1 C. shredded mozzarella cheese
20 slices pepperoni
½ C. chopped green pepper
1 small onion, chopped
Parmesan cheese

Directions

Cut 4 pieces of heavy-duty foil, each large enough to wrap around one chicken breast half with vegetables. Spray the foil with nonstick vegetable spray. Set 1 chicken breast half on each piece of foil. Spread ¼ cup pizza sauce over each piece of chicken. Sprinkle ¼ cup mozzarella cheese on top, followed by pepperoni slices, green pepper and onion, as desired. Press down on toppings slightly to hold them in place. Wrap foil in a tent pack around each serving. Cook as directed. Before serving, open packs and sprinkle Parmesan cheese on top.

Cooking Methods

 Preheat oven to 450°. Place foil packs on a baking sheet and bake for 18 to 25 minutes or until chicken is fully cooked.

 Place double-wrapped foil packs on medium embers and cook for 15 to 25 minutes or until chicken is fully cooked. Move packs as needed to obtain even heating.

 Preheat grill to medium-high heat. Place foil packs on the grill over direct heat, close lid and cook for 12 to 18 minutes or until chicken is fully cooked. Move packs as needed to obtain even heating.

Variations

• Add other favorite pizza toppings, such as sliced mushrooms and sliced black or green olives.

• Substitute spaghetti sauce for the pizza sauce and top the chicken with sliced zucchini, mozzarella cheese and Parmesan cheese.

• Substitute Alfredo-style pasta sauce for the pizza sauce and substitute sliced mushrooms for the other pizza toppings. Serve over cooked spaghetti or linguini.

Barbequed Chicken

Makes 4 servings

4 boneless, skinless chicken breast halves
1 C. barbeque sauce
1 (15.25 oz.) can whole kernel corn, drained
½ C. chopped green pepper

Directions

Cut 4 pieces of heavy-duty foil, each large enough to wrap around one chicken breast half with vegetables. Spray the foil with nonstick vegetable spray. Set 1 chicken breast half on each piece of foil. Spread about ¼ cup barbeque sauce on top of each chicken breast half. Spoon equal portions of the drained corn and green pepper on top of sauce. Wrap foil in a tent pack around each serving.

Cooking Methods

 Preheat oven to 450°. Place foil packs on a baking sheet and bake for 18 to 25 minutes or until chicken is fully cooked.

 Place double-wrapped foil packs on medium embers and cook for 15 to 25 minutes or until chicken is fully cooked. Move packs as needed to obtain even heating.

 Preheat grill to medium-high heat. Place foil packs on the grill over direct heat, close lid and cook for 12 to 18 minutes or until chicken is fully cooked. Move packs as needed to obtain even heating.

Variations

• Substitute chunky salsa for the barbeque sauce.

• Substitute sweet and sour sauce for the barbeque sauce and omit the corn and green pepper. Serve over rice.

Southwestern Chicken and Rice Dinner

Makes 4 servings

2 C. quick-cooking brown rice, uncooked
4 small boneless, skinless chicken breast halves
¼ C. ranch dressing (regular or reduced-calorie)
1½ tsp. chili powder
Cayenne pepper
½ C. shredded Cheddar cheese
4 C. fresh broccoli florets
1 medium red pepper, chopped

Directions

In a medium bowl, combine uncooked rice and 1¾ cups water. Let mixture stand for 5 minutes. Cut 4 pieces of heavy-duty foil, each large enough to wrap around 1 chicken breast half with vegetables. Spray foil with nonstick vegetable spray. Place equal portions of soaked rice on the center of each piece of foil. Place 1 chicken breast half on top. Sprinkle ½ teaspoon chili powder and a little cayenne pepper on each. Drizzle ranch dressing evenly over chicken. Place 2 tablespoons shredded cheese, 1 cup broccoli and a portion of the chopped red pepper on top. Wrap foil in a tent pack around each serving.

Cooking Methods

 Preheat oven to 400°. Place foil packs on a baking sheet and bake for 25 to 30 minutes or until chicken is fully cooked.

 Place double-wrapped foil packs on medium-hot embers and cook for 18 to 25 minutes or until chicken is fully cooked. Move packs several times during cooking to obtain even heating.

 Preheat grill to medium-high heat. Place foil packs on the grill over indirect heat, close lid and cook for 20 to 30 minutes or until chicken is fully cooked.

Variations

• Substitute white rice for the brown rice.

• Use frozen broccoli in place of fresh broccoli.

• For a milder chicken and rice dish, mix 2 cups quick-cooking white rice with 1 can cream of chicken soup. Stir in ½ cup water. Crimp foil edges to prevent spills. Spoon an even portion of rice mixture on each piece of foil and set 1 chicken breast half on top. Wrap and cook for 15 to 20 minutes on each side.

Tomato and Chicken Tortellini

Makes 2 servings

2 boneless, skinless chicken breast halves
½ tsp. dried Italian seasoning
1 (9 oz.) pkg. frozen cheese tortellini, thawed
1 (14.5 oz.) can diced tomatoes with basil, garlic
    and oregano, undrained
¼ C. sliced ripe olives

Directions

Cut 2 pieces of heavy-duty foil, each large enough to wrap
around 1 chicken breast half with tortellini. Spray the foil
pieces with nonstick vegetable spray. Place 1 chicken breast
on each piece of foil. Sprinkle Italian seasoning on top.
Arrange half of the tortellini around each piece of chicken
and top with half of the diced tomatoes. Sprinkle half of the
ripe olive slices on top of the tomatoes. Wrap foil in a tent
pack around each serving.

Cooking Methods

Preheat oven to 450°. Place foil packs on a baking sheet and bake for 25 to 30 minutes or until chicken is fully cooked.

Place double-wrapped foil packs on medium-hot embers and cook for 18 to 25 minutes or until chicken is fully cooked. Move packs as needed during cooking to obtain even heating.

Preheat grill to medium-high heat. Place foil packs on the grill over direct heat, close lid and cook for 14 to 22 minutes or until chicken is fully cooked.

Variations

• Substitute prepared spaghetti sauce for the diced tomatoes. Sprinkle with grated Parmesan cheese before serving.

• Substitute cheese ravioli for the tortellini.

Sweet Ham and Yams

Makes 4 servings

1 lb. boneless fully cooked ham
2 large yams or sweet potatoes
2 apples
Ground cinnamon
3 T. brown sugar
¼ C. pancake syrup

Directions

Cut ham into small chunks. Peel and cut yams into ½″ cubes.
Peel, core and cut each apple into 8 slices. Cut 4 (12″) pieces
of heavy-duty foil. Place an equal portion of ham and yam
chunks on each piece of foil. Place 4 apple slices on top of
each pack. Sprinkle each pack with cinnamon and 2 teaspoons
brown sugar, then drizzle 1 tablespoon syrup on top of each
serving. Wrap foil in a tent pack around each serving.

Cooking Methods

 Preheat oven to 350°. Place foil packs on a baking sheet and bake for 20 to 30 minutes or until yams are tender.

 Place double-wrapped foil packs on medium embers for 15 to 20 minutes or until yams are tender. Turn over after 10 minutes and move as needed to cook evenly.

 Preheat grill to medium heat. Place foil packs on the grill over direct heat, close lid and cook for 15 to 25 minutes or until yams are tender. Turn over once during cooking.

Variations

• Use drained, canned sweet potatoes in place of fresh yams. Reduce cooking time by 5 to 10 minutes.

• Use a ham slice instead of ham chunks and substitute crushed pineapple for the yams. Use $\frac{1}{8}$ teaspoon ground cloves in place of cinnamon. Wrap in a single foil pack and cook until ham is hot.

Pork Chops with Orange Glaze

Makes 4 servings

4 loin pork chops, ½″ thick
Salt and pepper
2 Granny Smith apples, peeled and thinly sliced
1 (29 oz.) can sweet potatoes in heavy syrup, drained
1 (10 oz.) jar orange marmalade
⅓ C. honey mustard

Directions

Cut 4 (18″) pieces of heavy-duty foil. Place 1 pork chop in the center of each piece of foil and sprinkle salt and pepper on top. Place an equal portion of sliced apples around each pork chop. Place an equal portion of sweet potatoes on top of each pork chop. In a small bowl, combine the orange marmalade and honey mustard. Mix well and spoon an equal portion over each pork chop. Wrap foil in a tent pack around each serving.

Cooking Methods

 Preheat oven to 450°. Place foil packs on a baking sheet and bake for 20 to 30 minutes or until pork chops are fully cooked.

 Place double-wrapped foil packs on medium embers for 15 to 20 minutes or until pork chops are fully cooked. Turn over after 10 minutes and move as needed to obtain even heating.

 Preheat grill to medium-high heat. Place foil packs on the grill over direct heat, close lid and cook for 13 to 20 minutes or until pork chops are fully cooked. Turn over after 10 minutes and move as needed to obtain even heating.

Variation

• Substitute cubed white or red potatoes for the sweet potatoes.

Teriyaki Pork Tenderloin

Makes 4 to 8 servings

1 to 1½ lbs. pork tenderloin
1 (1.27 oz.) pkg. dry onion soup mix
2 T. olive oil
Teriyaki sauce
2 apples, peeled and sliced
1 medium onion, sliced

Directions

Cut 2 pieces of heavy-duty foil large enough to wrap around the whole tenderloin. Stack the foil pieces and set the tenderloin in the center of the foil. Sprinkle the onion soup mix over the tenderloin and rub into the meat. Drizzle olive oil and some teriyaki sauce over meat. Top with apple and onion slices. Wrap foil pieces around tenderloin in a tent pack. Cook as directed. Let cooked meat stand for 10 to 15 minutes before slicing.

Cooking Methods

 Preheat oven to 325°. Place foil pack on a baking sheet and bake for about 1½ hours or until meat registers 155° to 160° on a meat thermometer and pork is tender.

 Place foil pack on medium embers for 50 to 70 minutes or until meat registers 155° to 160° on a meat thermometer and pork is tender. Turn every 15 minutes and move as needed to obtain even heating.

 Preheat grill to medium heat. Place foil pack on the grill over indirect heat, close lid and cook for 45 to 60 minutes or until meat registers 155° to 160° on a meat thermometer and pork is tender. Turn foil pack every 15 minutes.

Variations

• Start with plain tenderloin. In a small bowl, mix 1½ teaspoons each of garlic powder, chili powder, dry mustard, paprika and salt. Rub seasonings over all sides of the tenderloin and wrap in foil. If desired, brush with honey before serving.

• Start with plain tenderloin and brush with barbeque sauce before wrapping in foil.

Fish Fillets

Makes 4 servings

½ C. chopped onions
4 fish fillets (cod, orange roughy or haddock)
2 T. margarine, melted
¼ C. lemon juice
1 T. fresh chopped parsley
1 tsp. fresh dillweed
1 tsp. salt
¼ tsp. pepper
Paprika

Directions

Cut 4 pieces of heavy-duty foil, each large enough to wrap around 1 fish fillet. Place 2 tablespoons chopped onions on each piece of foil and top with a fish fillet. In a small bowl, mix melted margarine, lemon juice, parsley, dillweed, salt and pepper. Pour equal portions of the mixture over each fillet, then sprinkle with paprika. Wrap foil in a flat pack around each fillet.

Cooking Methods

Preheat oven to 425°. Place foil packs on a baking sheet and bake for 10 to 15 minutes, turning over once during cooking.

Wrap a second layer of foil around fish, twisting foil ends to make a 2-handle pack. Bury the fish packs in hot embers and cook for 8 to 15 minutes or until fish is white and flaky.

Preheat grill to medium-high heat. Place foil packs on the grill over direct heat and cook for 8 to 15 minutes, turning over once during cooking.

Variations

• Use whole fresh fish, like trout. Season the inside of the cleaned fish with salt and pepper. Add some chopped onions, chopped celery, chopped tomatoes and 1 tablespoon of margarine. Wrap in foil and cook as directed.

• In place of butter mixture, spoon prepared basil pesto over fillets and arrange sliced carrots around fish. Increase cooking time by 8 to 10 minutes.

• Turn this into a sandwich recipe by serving the cooked fish on a bun or hoagie with mayonnaise, Dijon mustard or tartar sauce. Add lettuce and tomato slices.

Glazed Salmon

Makes 2 servings

2 T. butter
½ C. brown sugar
1½ T. lemon juice
¾ tsp. dried dillweed
¼ tsp. cayenne pepper
2 frozen salmon fillets, partially thawed
Lemon pepper

Directions

In a small saucepan, melt butter. Add brown sugar, lemon juice, dillweed and cayenne pepper. Cook over low heat, stirring until brown sugar is dissolved. Cut 2 pieces of heavy-duty foil, each large enough to wrap around 1 salmon fillet. Spray foil pieces with nonstick vegetable spray. Place 1 salmon fillet on each piece of foil and brush each with half of the glaze. Wrap foil in a flat pack around each fillet.

Cooking Methods

 Preheat oven to 400°. Place foil packs on a baking sheet and bake for 17 to 22 minutes or until salmon flakes easily with a fork.

 Place double-wrapped foil packs on medium embers. Cook for 10 to 15 minutes or until salmon flakes easily with a fork. Move foil packs as needed to obtain even heating.

 Preheat grill to medium-high heat. Place foil packs on the grill over direct heat, close lid and cook for 8 to 15 minutes or until salmon flakes easily with a fork. Move packs as needed to obtain even heating.

Variation

- In place of the brown sugar mixture, combine ¼ cup honey, 2 tablespoons Dijon mustard, 1 tablespoon melted butter, 2 teaspoons Worcestershire sauce, 1 tablespoon cornstarch and a dash of pepper. Spread this sauce over the salmon before wrapping in foil.

Spicy Shrimp

Makes 4 servings

1 to 1½ lbs. large shrimp, peeled and deveined
Salt and pepper
1½ C. chunky salsa
1 tsp. garlic powder
¾ tsp. crushed red pepper flakes
1 (16 oz.) can whole green beans, drained
Italian-seasoned grated Parmesan cheese

Directions

Cut 4 pieces of heavy-duty foil, each large enough to hold
1 serving of shrimp and green beans. Spray foil with nonstick
vegetable spray. Place an equal portion of the shrimp on each
piece of foil. Sprinkle shrimp with salt and pepper. In a small
bowl, combine salsa, garlic powder and red pepper flakes.
Spoon the salsa mixture evenly over shrimp. Arrange some
green beans next to shrimp on each piece of foil. Wrap foil
around shrimp in a tent pack and cook as directed. Before
serving, sprinkle cooked shrimp with Parmesan cheese.

Cooking Methods

Preheat oven to 450°. Place foil packs on a baking sheet and bake for 15 to 20 minutes or until shrimp is fully cooked.

Place double-wrapped foil packs on medium-hot embers. Cook for 8 to 12 minutes or until shrimp is fully cooked. Move foil packs as needed to obtain even heating.

Preheat grill to medium-high heat. Place foil packs on the grill over direct heat, close lid and cook for 8 to 15 minutes or until shrimp is fully cooked.

Variations

• Substitute frozen broccoli florets or fresh snow peas for the green beans and use ½ cup soy sauce in place of salsa. Omit red pepper flakes and Parmesan cheese. Serve over rice.

• Make Garlic Shrimp by mixing ½ cup softened butter with garlic powder and some minced parsley. Omit vegetables, salsa, red pepper flakes and Parmesan cheese. Spoon an equal portion of butter mixture on top of each shrimp pack and cook as directed.

Potatoes & Other Vegetables

Quick and easy side dishes to love!

Potato & Vegetable Cooking Tips

- *Potatoes and other starchy vegetables may stick to foil, so spray the foil with a nonstick vegetable spray before adding these foods, or purchase nonstick foil.*

- *It takes longer to cook large pieces of potatoes or other vegetables. To speed up cooking time, cut vegetables into smaller cubes or thin slices.*

- *For faster cooking, use canned vegetables in place of fresh or frozen ones.*

- *Frozen vegetables add moisture to a foil pack. If additional moisture is desired, add 1 or 2 ice cubes.*

- *Bend foil edges up and crimp them slightly before adding liquid ingredients to foil packs. Then seal tightly to hold in liquids*

- *When cooking in foil packs, it is usually best to add fresh cheese after cooking, unless otherwise directed.*

- *Leave the peel on vegetables that lose their shape when cooked, such as zucchini or eggplant.*

- *When cooking a variety of vegetables in one foil pack, allow enough time for those vegetables that require the longest cooking time.*

- *It is convenient to combine dry ingredients and seasonings in a ziplock baggie at home before leaving on a camping trip rather than packing each individual ingredient.*

- *Fresh potatoes should be sliced just before cooking to prevent browning. Most other vegetables can be sliced ahead of time.*

Basic Potatoes in Foil

Makes 2 to 4 servings

2 large potatoes
1 to 2 medium onions
Salt and pepper
Garlic powder
2 T. butter, cut into pieces

Directions

Cut 1 piece of heavy-duty foil 15″ long. Spray foil with
nonstick vegetable spray. Peel and slice the potatoes. Cut
onions into small pieces. Place potatoes and onions on foil.
Sprinkle with salt, pepper and garlic powder to taste. Arrange
pieces of butter over vegetables. Wrap foil around vegetables
in a tent pack.

Cooking Methods

 Preheat oven to 375°. Place foil pack on a baking sheet and bake for 30 to 40 minutes or until potatoes are tender.

 Place double-wrapped foil pack on medium embers and cook for 20 to 30 minutes or until potatoes are tender. Turn pack over several times during cooking.

 Preheat grill to medium heat. Place foil pack on the grill over direct heat, close lid and cook for 15 to 25 minutes or until potatoes are tender. Turn pack over several times during cooking.

Variations

• Use 4 large potatoes and substitute 1 package dry onion soup mix for the onions and seasonings. Layer half the potatoes, some butter and half the onion soup mix on sprayed foil. Make a second layer of all three ingredients, wrap in foil and cook as directed.

• Before serving, sprinkle grated Cheddar or mozarella cheese on top of hot potatoes and let cheese melt.

Herbed New Potatoes

Makes 8 servings

⅓ C. olive oil
2 lbs. new potatoes
½ medium yellow onion or sweet Spanish onion
½ tsp. dried rosemary
¾ tsp. salt
½ tsp. pepper
Pinch of cayenne pepper

Directions

Cut 8 (10˝) pieces of heavy-duty foil. Brush each piece with olive oil. Wash and slice the potatoes about ¼˝ thick. Place an equal portion of sliced potatoes on each piece of foil. Slice the onion into rings about ¼˝ thick. Separate the rings and place an equal portion on top of the potatoes in each pack. Sprinkle vegetables with rosemary, salt, pepper and cayenne pepper. Crimp foil edges enough to hold in liquids. Drizzle vegetables with remaining olive oil. Wrap foil in a tent pack around each serving.

Cooking Methods

 Preheat oven to 400°. Place foil packs on a baking sheet and bake for 25 to 35 minutes or until potatoes are tender.

 Place double-wrapped foil packs on medium embers and cook for 15 to 20 minutes or until potatoes are tender. Turn packs over several times during cooking.

 Preheat grill to medium-high heat. Place foil packs on the grill over direct heat, close lid and cook for 15 to 25 minutes or until potatoes are tender. Turn packs over several times during cooking.

Variations

• Combine ingredients into a single large foil pack and add 4 cloves finely chopped garlic with the other seasonings. Before serving, sprinkle ½ cup shredded Parmesan cheese on hot potatoes.

• To make Lemony New Potatoes, omit onions, rosemary leaves and cayenne pepper. Place all potatoes on 1 large piece of foil, crimping edges enough to hold in liquids. Sprinkle with ½ teaspoon celery salt, 1 teaspoon dillweed, salt and pepper. Drizzle remaining olive oil on top. Mix ¼ cup lemon juice with ¼ cup water. Pour the liquid over potatoes and seal tent pack well before cooking. Increase cooking time slightly.

Mushroom-Stuffed Hash Browns

Makes 2 servings

4 frozen hash brown potato patties
Soft margarine
Seasoned salt
1 (4 oz.) can mushrooms, drained

Directions

Cut 1 piece of heavy-duty foil large enough to hold all
4 hash brown patties. Spread margarine on both sides of
2 hash brown patties. Place them side by side on the foil,
margarine side up. Spread drained mushrooms over the
patties. Sprinkle seasoned salt on top. Spread margarine on
both sides of the remaining hash brown patties and place
them on top, sandwich style. Wrap foil in a flat pack.

Cooking Methods

 Preheat oven to 400°. Place foil pack on a baking sheet. Bake for 15 to 20 minutes or until hash browns are soft and heated through.

 Place double-wrapped foil pack on medium embers and cook for 10 to 20 minutes or until hash browns are soft and heated through. Turn pack over once during cooking.

 Preheat grill to medium-high heat. Place foil pack on the grill over direct heat, close lid and cook for 12 to 18 minutes or until hash browns are soft and heated through. Turn pack over once during cooking.

Variations

• Place thinly sliced onions or green bell peppers between hash brown patties before cooking.

• Place sliced processed cheese on top of hot hash browns just before serving.

Southwestern Potato Pack

Makes 4 servings

4 medium potatoes
1 medium onion, thinly sliced
1 tsp. seasoned salt
½ tsp. chili powder
¼ tsp. ground cumin
1 (4.5 oz.) can chopped green chilies, undrained
1 C. shredded Cheddar cheese
Salsa
Chopped fresh cilantro
Sour cream

Directions

Cut 1 piece of foil large enough to hold all the vegetables. Spray foil with nonstick vegetable spray. Peel and cut the potatoes into ½″ cubes. Place the sliced onions on the foil. Arrange potatoes on top of onions. In a small bowl, combine the seasoned salt, chili powder and cumin. Sprinkle spice mixture over potatoes. Spoon the chopped green chilies on top. Wrap foil around vegetables in a tent pack and cook as directed. After potatoes are cooked, open the pack and sprinkle with shredded Cheddar cheese. After cheese melts, serve potatoes with salsa, cilantro and sour cream.

Cooking Methods

 Preheat oven to 450°. Place foil pack on a baking sheet and bake for 25 to 35 minutes or until potatoes are tender.

 Place double-wrapped foil pack on medium-hot embers and cook for 20 to 30 minutes or until potatoes are tender. Turn pack over several times during cooking.

 Preheat grill to medium-high heat. Place foil pack on the grill over direct heat, close lid and cook for 15 to 25 minutes or until potatoes are tender. Turn pack over several times during cooking.

Variation

• Make quick Tex-Mex Potatoes by replacing the seasoned salt, chili powder and cumin with ½ envelope dry taco seasoning. Mix the seasoning into the potatoes before wrapping in foil.

Easy Cheesy Potatoes and Peas

Makes 4 servings

4 medium potatoes
1 (10 oz.) pkg. frozen peas
½ tsp. pepper
1 (16 oz.) jar pasteurized processed cheese sauce

Directions

Wash and cut the potatoes into ¼″ slices. Cut 4 (18″) pieces of heavy-duty foil. Spray foil pieces with nonstick vegetable spray. Place an equal portion of sliced potatoes on each piece of foil. Top with an equal portion of peas. Sprinkle pepper on top. Spoon desired amount of cheese sauce over vegetables in each pack. Wrap foil in a tent pack around each serving.

Cooking Methods

 Preheat oven to 450°. Place foil packs on a baking sheet and bake for 25 to 35 minutes or until potatoes are tender.

 Place double-wrapped foil packs on medium-hot embers and cook for 15 to 25 minutes or until potatoes are tender. Rotate packs several times during cooking.

 Preheat grill to medium-high heat. Place foil pack on the grill over direct heat, close lid and cook for 8 to 15 minutes or until potatoes are tender. Rotate packs several times during cooking.

Variation

• For a main dish, add 12 ounces fully-cooked, cubed ham to mixture before wrapping in foil. Increase cooking time slightly.

Potato and Zucchini Medley

Makes 6 to 8 servings

1 onion, peeled and quartered
12 baby new potatoes, scrubbed and quartered
4 medium zucchini, cut into 1″ chunks
2 T. olive oil
2 cloves garlic, sliced
1 tsp. dried rosemary
½ tsp. paprika
1 tsp. salt
½ tsp. pepper

Directions

In a large bowl, combine the quartered onions, potatoes and zucchini. Drizzle with olive oil and toss until evenly coated. Add sliced garlic, rosemary, paprika, salt and pepper; stir well. Cut 1 piece of heavy-duty foil large enough to wrap around all the vegetables. Spray foil with nonstick vegetable spray and place vegetables on top. Wrap foil around vegetables in a tent pack.

Cooking Methods

 Preheat oven to 425°. Place foil pack on a baking sheet and bake for 20 to 25 minutes or until potatoes are tender.

 Place a grate on top of the fire close to the hot coals. Cook foil pack on grate for 18 to 25 minutes or until potatoes are tender. Rotate pack several times during cooking.

 Preheat grill to medium-high heat. Place foil pack on the grill over direct heat, close lid and cook for 15 to 25 minutes or until potatoes are tender. Rotate pack several times during cooking.

Variation

• Use a peeled and thinly sliced sweet potato and ½ pound fresh green beans in place of the zucchini. Add a sprig of fresh thyme.

Broccoli Casserole

Makes 4 servings

6 C. broccoli florets
1 (10.75 oz.) can cream of mushroom soup
¼ C. mayonnaise
1 T. Worcestershire sauce
Salt and pepper
½ C. shredded Cheddar cheese
⅔ C. dry, seasoned bread stuffing mix

Directions

Cut 1 piece of wide heavy-duty foil 24˝ long. Spray foil with nonstick vegetable spray. Place broccoli in the middle of foil. Crimp foil edges enough to hold in liquids. In a small bowl, combine the soup, mayonnaise, Worcestershire sauce, salt and pepper; mix well. Pour mixture over broccoli. Sprinkle cheese over broccoli and top with stuffing mix. Wrap foil around broccoli in a tent pack.

Cooking Methods

 Preheat oven to 450°. Place foil pack on a baking sheet and bake for 18 to 24 minutes or until broccoli is tender.

 Place double-wrapped foil pack on medium-hot embers and cook for 10 to 20 minutes or until broccoli is tender. Turn pack several times during cooking.

 Preheat grill to medium-high heat. Place foil pack on the grill over direct heat, close lid and cook for 10 to 14 minutes or until broccoli is tender. Turn pack several times during cooking.

Variation

• Substitute cauliflower florets for the broccoli or use a combination of the two vegetables.

Citrus Broccoli and Carrots

Makes 6 to 8 servings

¼ C. orange marmalade
½ tsp. salt
1½ C. baby carrots
6 C. broccoli florets
1 (11 oz.) can mandarin oranges, drained
¼ C. cashews

Directions

In a large bowl, mix orange marmalade with salt. Cut each carrot in half lengthwise. Add the carrots and broccoli to marmalade mixture and stir well to coat. Cut 1 piece of wide heavy-duty foil 24˝ long. Spray foil with nonstick vegetable spray. Place vegetable mixture in the middle of the foil piece. Wrap foil around vegetables in a tent pack. Cook as directed. After cooking, open pack and stir in mandarin oranges. Sprinkle cashews on top before serving.

Cooking Methods

 Preheat oven to 450°. Place foil pack on a baking sheet and bake for 15 to 20 minutes or until vegetables are tender.

 Place double-wrapped foil pack on medium embers and cook for 8 to 15 minutes or until vegetables are tender. Rotate pack several times during cooking.

 Preheat grill to medium-high heat. Place foil pack on the grill over direct heat, close lid and cook for 8 to 12 minutes or until vegetables are tender. Rotate pack several times during cooking.

Variation

• Sprinkle cooked vegetables with toasted slivered almonds or pine nuts in place of the cashews.

Artichokes and Carrots

Makes 6 servings

8 carrots
1 (15 oz.) can artichoke hearts
Juice of 1 lemon
1 T. sugar
¼ C. butter, melted
2 T. chopped parsley
1 tsp. salt
Pepper

Directions

Peel carrots and cut them into strips. Drain artichoke hearts and cut each into 4 pieces. In a small bowl, combine lemon juice, sugar, melted butter, parsley, salt and pepper. Stir to mix well. Cut 6 (12˝) squares of heavy-duty foil. Place equal portions of the carrots and artichokes on each piece. Crimp edges of foil enough to hold in liquids. Pour an equal portion of the butter mixture over vegetables. Wrap foil in a tent pack around each serving.

Cooking Methods

 Preheat oven to 350°. Place foil packs on a baking sheet and bake for 20 to 30 minutes or until carrots are tender.

 Place double-wrapped foil packs on medium embers for 18 to 25 minutes or until carrots are tender. Rotate pack several times during cooking.

 Preheat grill to medium heat. Place foil packs on the grill over direct heat, close lid and cook for 15 to 25 minutes or until carrots are tender. Rotate pack several times during cooking.

Variation

• Substitute asparagus spears for the artichoke hearts.

Candied Carrots

Makes 5 to 6 servings

¾ C. brown sugar
1 T. ground cinnamon
1 T. sugar
Pinch of salt
1 (1 lb.) pkg. baby carrots
2 to 3 T. butter or margarine

Directions

In a medium bowl, combine the brown sugar, cinnamon,
sugar and salt; mix well. Cut 1 piece of heavy-duty foil
large enough to wrap around all the carrots. Spray foil with
nonstick vegetable spray. Place carrots on foil. Sprinkle sugar
mixture on carrots and arrange pieces of butter on top. Wrap
foil around carrots in a tent pack.

Cooking Methods

Preheat oven to 375°. Place foil pack on a baking sheet and bake for 20 to 25 minutes or until carrots are tender.

Place double-wrapped foil pack on medium embers and cook for 12 to 20 minutes or until carrots are tender. Rotate pack several times during cooking.

Preheat grill to medium heat. Place foil pack on the grill over direct heat, close lid and cook for 12 to 18 minutes or until carrots are tender. Rotate pack several times during cooking.

Variation

• Make Honeyed Carrots by sprinkling 2 tablespoons brown sugar over plain carrots on the foil. Drizzle with 2 tablespoons honey and top with 2 tablespoons butter.

Corn on the Cob

Makes 4 servings

4 ears sweet corn
4 T. butter or margarine, softened
Salt, optional

Directions

Peel back husks and remove silk from the sweet corn but leave a few layers of husk attached. Rinse corn with cool water. Spread the butter or margarine on the corn. Sprinkle with salt, if desired. Fold corn husks back over the corn and wrap each piece tightly in 1 piece of heavy-duty foil. After cooking as directed, carefully unwrap foil and peel off the husks.

Cooking Methods

 Preheat oven to 375°. Place foil-wrapped corn on a jellyroll pan and bake for 20 to 30 minutes or until corn is tender. Turn occasionally during cooking.

 Wrap each piece of corn in another sheet of foil, and twist it at each end to make a 2-handled pack. Bury wrapped corn in medium embers for 15 to 30 minutes or until corn is tender.

 Preheat grill to medium heat. Place wrapped corn on the grill over indirect heat, close lid and cook for 15 to 25 minutes or until corn is tender. Turn occasionally during cooking.

Variations

• Before wrapping, sprinkle corn with Cajun seasoning or garlic powder.

• Substitute butter-flavored spray, butter substitute sprinkles and garlic powder for the butter and salt.

• Corn husks may be completely removed before cooking. Brush the corn with butter and/or seasonings, set 2 ice cubes on top and wrap the ears together in 1 foil pack. Cook a bit longer than directed.

• For a spicy kick, combine ½ cup melted butter with 2 tablespoons Dijon mustard, 1 tablespoon minced fresh parsley, 2 teaspoons prepared horseradish, ½ teaspoon salt and pepper to taste. Brush the mixture over the corn, wrap and cook as directed.

83

Asian Asparagus

Makes 3 to 4 servings

2 T. olive oil or sesame oil
Dash of cayenne pepper
1 tsp. brown sugar
2 tsp. soy sauce
1 lb. fresh asparagus spears, trimmed

Directions

In a medium bowl, combine the olive oil, cayenne pepper, brown sugar and soy sauce. Add the asparagus and toss together until well coated. Cut 1 piece of foil large enough to wrap around asparagus. Spray foil with nonstick vegetable spray. Crimp foil edges enough to hold in liquids. Place coated asparagus on foil. Wrap foil around asparagus in a tent pack.

Cooking Methods

Preheat oven to 375°. Place foil pack on a baking sheet and bake for 15 to 20 minutes or until asparagus is tender.

Place double-wrapped foil pack on warm embers and cook for 10 to 15 minutes or until asparagus is tender. Rotate pack several times during cooking.

Preheat grill to medium heat. Place foil pack on the grill over direct heat, close lid and cook for 15 to 20 minutes or until asparagus is tender. Rotate pack several times during cooking.

Variations

- Add minced garlic to taste. Before serving, sprinkle with toasted sesame seeds.

- This recipe can also be grilled in an open foil pack on an outdoor grill. Wrap 2 layers of foil around the bottom of a baking dish, crimping edges to make a sturdy foil pan. Remove baking dish. Place asparagus in foil pan and cook uncovered for 10 to 15 minutes or until crisp tender. Use long tongs to turn asparagus during cooking.

- Cook plain asparagus with 2 tablespoons butter or margarine in a foil pack but omit the other seasonings. Prepare a mustard cream sauce to serve over the cooked asparagus. In a microwave-safe bowl, combine 1 cup sour cream with 2 tablespoons red wine vinegar, ¼ cup Dijon mustard, 2 teaspoons sugar and ⅛ teaspoon crushed red pepper flakes. Microwave on high for 1½ minutes or until warm. Drizzle over cooked asparagus.

Cauliflower with Spicy Cheese Sauce

Makes 4 servings

4 C. cauliflower florets
4 oz. pasteurized processed cheese sauce
1 tsp. hot pepper sauce
¼ tsp. crushed red pepper flakes, optional

Directions

Cut 1 piece of foil large enough to wrap around all the cauliflower. Spray foil with nonstick vegetable spray. Place cauliflower pieces in the center of foil. In a small bowl, mix the cheese sauce, hot pepper sauce and red pepper flakes. Spread cheese sauce over the cauliflower. Wrap foil around cauliflower in a tent pack.

Cooking Methods

 Preheat oven to 450°. Place foil pack on a baking sheet and bake for 20 to 30 minutes or until cauliflower is tender.

 Place double-wrapped foil pack on medium-hot embers and cook for 8 to 15 minutes or until cauliflower is tender. Rotate pack several times during cooking.

 Preheat grill to medium heat. Place foil pack on the grill, close lid and cook for 8 to 15 minutes or until cauliflower is tender. Rotate pack several times during cooking.

Variation

• Omit cheese sauce, hot pepper sauce and red pepper flakes. Combine cauliflower with ½ cup sun-dried tomatoes, 3 tablespoons olive oil, 2 cloves minced garlic and 1 teaspoon dried basil. Place on foil, sprinkle ⅓ cup grated Parmesan over vegetables and add 4 ice cubes to the pack before sealing. Cook as directed.

Sandwiches

Beyond the burger – simply great sandwiches!

Sandwich Cooking Tips

- *Hamburger patties cooked in foil will not brown well or become crisp on the outside since they are cooked by steam. Don't be alarmed, as the beef will still lose most of its pink color when fully cooked.*

- *The safest way to check for doneness is to use a quick-read meat thermometer. The thermometer should be inserted horizontally into the side of ground meat patties to check internal temperatures.*

- *Be careful not to overcook meat. If a foil pack is placed on coals that are too hot, the meat can become crusty and tough.*

- *Double-wrap sandwiches that will be cooked directly in a campfire.*

- *If the sandwich ingredients are pre-cooked before wrapping in foil packs, heat the packs just until sandwich fillings are hot.*

- *When using flour tortillas, warm them until they are soft and pliable before rolling them around sandwich fillings. You may wrap tortillas flat in a piece of foil and warm them with low heat using an oven, campfire or grill. They may also be placed on a paper plate or wrapped in paper towels and warmed for a few seconds in a microwave oven.*

Pizza Burger

Makes 4 servings

1 lb. lean ground beef
1 egg
¼ C. grated Parmesan cheese
¼ C. finely chopped onion
½ tsp. dried basil
½ tsp. dried oregano
½ tsp. dried rosemary
¼ tsp. fennel seeds, optional
Salt and pepper, optional
4 slices provolone
4 English muffins
¼ to ½ C. prepared pizza sauce

Directions

In a large bowl, combine meat, egg, Parmesan cheese, onion, basil, oregano, rosemary, fennel seeds, salt and pepper. Shape mixture into 4 equal-sized patties, about ¾" thick. Cut 4 (14") pieces of heavy-duty foil. Wrap foil around each patty in a flat pack. While patties cook, toast the English muffins in a toaster or on a grill. After cooking the patties as directed, open the foil and set 1 slice of cheese on top of each patty. Meanwhile, spread some pizza sauce on each muffin half. Remove each patty from foil and place between a pair of toasted muffin halves.

Cooking Methods

 Preheat oven to 350°. Place foil packs on a baking sheet and bake for 20 minutes or until hamburger is fully cooked.

 Place double-wrapped foil packs on hot coals and cook for 8 to 15 minutes or until hamburger is fully cooked. Turn packs over once during cooking.

 Preheat grill to medium heat. Place foil packs on the grill over direct heat, close lid and cook for 12 to 18 minutes or until hamburgers are fully cooked. Turn packs over once during cooking.

Variations

- Substitute shredded or sliced mozzarella cheese for the provolone.

- Serve on hamburger buns instead of English muffins.

- Omit the English muffins and serve burgers alone as the main dish, placing a large spoonful of warmed pizza sauce on top of the cheese.

Zippy Hot Ham and Cheese Sandwiches

Makes 4 servings

3 T. butter, softened
1½ T. prepared horseradish mustard
1 T. minced onions
½ tsp. poppy seeds
½ tsp. dillseed
4 hamburger buns
4 slices Swiss cheese
8 thin ham slices

Directions

In a small bowl, combine butter, mustard, onions, poppy seeds and dillseed. Spread an equal amount of the butter mixture on insides of each bun half. Place 1 slice of cheese and 2 slices of ham on the bottom half of each bun. Cover with bun tops. Cut 4 (12″) pieces of heavy-duty foil. Wrap foil around each sandwich in a flat pack.

Cooking Methods

Preheat oven to 350°. Place foil packs on the center rack and bake for 10 to 15 minutes or until cheese melts.

Place double-wrapped foil packs on warm embers and cook for 10 to 15 minutes or until cheese melts. Move packs as needed to obtain even heating.

Preheat grill to low heat. Place foil packs on the grill over indirect heat, close lid and cook for 10 to 20 minutes or until cheese melts. Move packs as needed to obtain even heating.

Variations

• Use American, Cheddar or provolone cheese in place of Swiss cheese.

• Substitute mayonnaise for the butter spread. Place very thin slices of fresh apple and mozzarella cheese on top of ham, wrap and cook as directed above.

Hot Sourdough Deli Sandwiches

Makes 4 servings

8 slices sourdough bread
5 to 6 oz. thinly sliced deli ham
5 to 6 oz. thinly sliced smoked turkey
5 to 6 oz. thinly sliced pastrami
4 thin slices sweet onion
⅔ C. sliced fresh mushrooms
⅔ C. sliced green bell peppers
4 slices bacon, cooked and crumbled
4 slices provolone cheese

Directions

On 4 slices of bread, layer equal portions of ham, turkey
and pastrami slices. Place 1 slice of onion, a few mushrooms
and some green peppers on top of the meat. Sprinkle with
crumbled bacon and add 1 slice of provolone cheese. Cover
each with a remaining slice of bread. Cut 4 (14˝) pieces
of heavy-duty foil. Wrap foil around each sandwich in a
flat pack.

Cooking Methods

 Preheat oven to 350°. Place foil packs on the center rack and bake for 10 to 15 minutes or until sandwiches are heated through.

 Place double-wrapped foil packs on medium-hot embers and cook for 8 to 10 minutes or until sandwiches are heated through. Turn packs over once during cooking.

 Preheat grill to medium heat. Place foil packs on the grill over indirect heat and close lid. Cook for 10 to 15 minutes or until sandwiches are heated through. Turn packs over once during cooking.

Variations

• After cooking, add various condiments, such as Dijon mustard, yellow mustard, mayonnaise, lettuce and sliced tomatoes.

• Try other cheese combinations such as American, Swiss and/or Monterey Jack.

• Before assembling sandwiches, sauté the vegetables in a little olive oil until tender. Place sautéed vegetables on sandwiches, wrap and cook as directed.

Brats with Seasoned Sauerkraut

Makes 4 servings

⅓ C. chopped green bell pepper
¼ C. chopped onion
1½ T. brown sugar
1 tsp. yellow mustard
½ tsp. caraway seed
¾ C. drained sauerkraut
4 fully-cooked bratwursts
4 hoagie buns or large hot dog buns

Directions

In a medium bowl, combine the chopped green pepper and onion. Stir in the brown sugar, mustard, caraway seed and drained sauerkraut. Mix well. Cut 2 (16″) pieces of heavy-duty foil. Stack foil pieces together. Spray top layer with nonstick vegetable spray. Spoon the seasoned sauerkraut in the center of the foil. Grill the brats by themselves over the fire or arrange them on top of the sauerkraut and fold foil into a tent pack. After cooking as directed, place 1 brat on each bun and spoon sauerkraut on top.

Cooking Methods

 Preheat oven to 375°. Cook the brats inside the foil pack with the sauerkraut. Set foil pack on a baking sheet. Bake for 20 to 25 minutes or until heated through

 Use medium-hot coals and cook brats by themselves over direct heat on a grill or with long campfire forks. Turn brats several times during cooking. Place double-wrapped pack of sauerkraut on warm embers for 15 to 20 minutes or until heated through.

 Preheat grill to medium heat. Place brats on the grill above direct heat and set pack of sauerkraut to the side or back over indirect heat. Close lid and cook for 15 to 20 minutes or until brats are cooked and sauerkraut is heated through. Turn brats several times during cooking.

Variations

- Sauté the onion and green bell pepper in a skillet with 2 tablespoons olive oil before assembling sandwiches.

- Wrap brats in their own foil pack to cook in the oven.

Wrapped Tuna Melts

Makes 4 servings

1 (12 oz.) can tuna in water, drained
2 C. cooked rice
1 C. frozen green peas
½ C. mayonnaise
1 T. lemon pepper
1½ C. shredded Cheddar cheese, divided
4 (10˝) flour tortillas, warmed

Directions

Cut 4 (16˝) pieces of heavy-duty foil. In a medium bowl, combine drained tuna, cooked rice, peas, mayonnaise, lemon pepper and 1 cup cheese; mix well. Spread an equal portion of tuna mixture across the center of each warm tortilla. Fold and roll up tortillas, enclosing the filling like a burrito. Place each rolled tortilla on a piece of foil with seam side down. Wrap foil around each tortilla in a flat pack. After cooking, sprinkle remaining shredded cheese on top of tortillas.

Cooking Methods

 Preheat oven to 350°. Place foil packs on a baking sheet and bake for 15 to 22 minutes or until heated through.

 Place double-wrapped foil packs on medium-hot embers and cook for 8 to 10 minutes. Turn packs over once during cooking.

 Preheat grill to medium-high heat. Place foil packs to the side of the grill over indirect heat. Close lid and cook for 8 to 10 minutes or until heated through. Turn packs over once during cooking.

Variations

• Substitute canned chicken or ham for the tuna.

• Add ½ cup finely chopped celery.

Crab and Cheese Sandwiches

Makes 4 servings

2 (6 oz.) cans crab meat
½ C. shredded Cheddar cheese
¼ C. minced onion
¼ C. mayonnaise
1 T. lemon juice
½ tsp. seasoned salt
½ tsp. dillweed
¼ tsp. dry mustard
4 large dinner rolls
2 T. soft butter, optional

Directions

Drain the crab meat. In a medium bowl, mix the crab meat, cheese and minced onion. In a separate bowl, combine the mayonnaise, lemon juice, seasoned salt, dillweed and dry mustard; mix well. Stir the dressing into the crab mixture. Split rolls and hollow out part of the center of each roll half. If desired, spread buns with butter. Spoon ¼ of the crab mixture into each bun bottom. Replace bun tops. Cut 4 pieces of heavy-duty foil, each large enough to wrap around 1 sandwich. Wrap foil around each filled sandwich in a flat pack.

Cooking Methods

 Preheat oven to 350°. Place foil packs on a baking sheet and bake for 18 to 22 minutes or until cheese melts.

 Place double-wrapped foil packs on warm embers and cook for 15 to 20 minutes or until cheese melts. Turn packs over halfway through cooking and move as needed to obtain even heating.

 Preheat grill to medium heat. Place foil packs on the grill over direct heat and close lid. Cook for 15 to 20 minutes or until cheese melts, turning once halfway through cooking.

Variations

• Substitute canned lobster meat for the crab meat.

• Substitute Swiss cheese for the Cheddar cheese.

• Substitute large hamburger buns or croissants for the dinner rolls.

Meatball Subs

Makes 4 servings

1 lb. frozen, fully cooked Italian-style meatballs
1 (27 oz.) jar chunky spaghetti sauce
4 hoagie-style rolls
1 C. shredded mozzarella cheese

Directions

Cut 4 (16″) pieces of heavy-duty foil. Place ¼ of the frozen meatballs on each piece of foil. Top with desired amount of spaghetti sauce. Wrap foil around each serving of meatballs in a flat pack. Cook as directed. Before serving, spoon meatballs on hoagie rolls and sprinkle shredded cheese on top.

Cooking Methods

Preheat oven to 450°. Place foil packs on a baking sheet and bake for 15 to 20 minutes or until heated through.

Place double-wrapped foil packs on medium embers and cook for 10 to 20 minutes, or until heated through. Turn packs over once during cooking.

Preheat grill to medium-high heat. Place foil packs on the grill over direct heat, close lid and cook for 10 to 12 minutes or until heated through. Turn packs over once during cooking.

Variation

• Place all meatballs into 1 foil pack and heat them together. Increase cooking time as needed until meatballs and sauce are fully heated.

Grilled Beef Fajitas

Makes 4 servings

1 lb. boneless beef sirloin steak
1 (1.27 oz.) pkg. fajita seasoning mix
1 green bell pepper, sliced
1 red or yellow bell pepper, sliced
1 medium onion, sliced
1 to 2 T. olive oil
4 (10˝) flour tortillas, warmed
Salsa

Directions

Slice steak into thin strips. In a medium bowl, prepare fajita seasoning mix with water according to package instructions. Add steak strips, cover bowl and refrigerate for 1 to 2 hours to let steak marinate. Stir several times.

Cut 1 (18˝) square piece of heavy-duty foil. Place the sliced green and red bell peppers and onions in the center of the foil. Drizzle olive oil on top. Remove the steak strips from bowl, discarding marinade. Arrange the sliced steak in a single layer on top of the vegetables. Wrap foil around food in a tent pack. Cook as directed. After the foil pack is cooked, spoon the hot steak mixture on warm tortillas, roll them up and serve with salsa.

Cooking Methods

Preheat oven to 450°. Place fajita foil pack on a baking sheet and bake for 13 to 18 minutes or until steak is fully cooked and vegetables are tender.

Double-wrap the fajita foil pack, making a 2-handled pack with the second layer of foil. Bury the foil pack in medium embers and cook for 10 to 20 minutes or until steak is fully cooked and vegetables are tender.

Preheat grill to medium-high heat. Place fajita foil pack on the grill over direct heat, close lid and cook for 8 to 12 minutes or until steak is fully cooked and vegetables are tender. Turn pack over once during cooking.

Variation

• Substitute sliced boneless, skinless chicken breast for the beef steak.

Rice and Bean Burritos

Makes 4 servings

1 (16 oz.) can refried beans
1⅓ C. cooked rice
1⅓ C. shredded Cheddar cheese
1⅓ C. salsa
⅓ C. chopped green onion
2 T. chopped fresh cilantro
4 (10˝) flour tortillas, warmed

Directions

In a medium bowl, combine the refried beans, cooked rice, cheese, salsa, green onion and cilantro. Mix well and set aside. Cut 4 (18˝) pieces of heavy-duty foil. Place 1 tortilla on each piece of foil. Spoon equal portions of the bean and rice mixture across the middle of each tortilla. Roll the tortillas burrito-style and set them seam side down on the foil. Wrap foil around each burrito in a flat pack.

Cooking Methods

 Preheat oven to 450°. Place foil packs on a baking sheet and bake for 18 to 20 minutes or until burritos are heated through.

 Set double-wrapped foil packs on medium embers and cook for 10 to 15 minutes or until heated through. Turn packs over every 5 minutes.

 Preheat grill to medium-high heat. Place foil packs on the grill over direct heat, close lid and cook for 12 to 16 minutes or until heated through. Turn packs over once during cooking.

Variation

• In a medium skillet, brown ½ pound ground beef with ½ envelope taco seasoning. Add water as directed on the package. Add the cooked meat to the rice and bean mixture before spreading it over 6 tortillas. Wrap and cook as directed.

Desserts
Tasty endings to any meal!

Dessert Cooking Tips

• *Desserts containing sugar and fats, such as chocolate, caramel and marshmallows, will be very hot after being cooked in foil. Handle and unwrap these items carefully using oven mitts. Let them cool a bit before serving.*

• *If making a dessert using flour tortillas, wrap the tortillas flat in foil and heat them for a few minutes in the oven or on a grill to make them pliable. They can also be placed on paper plates or wrapped in paper towels and warmed in a microwave oven. Do not place foil in the microwave.*

• *When cooking food in a foil pan, set pan on a baking sheet to transport it to and from the campfire or grill. Slide it off the baking sheet onto the grill.*

• *Use an oven mitt and gently squeeze the sides of a foil-wrapped apple to check for doneness. Apple will feel soft when fully cooked.*

• *Fruit desserts and those using cake mixes are best if assembled just before cooking.*

Basic Baked Apple

Makes 1 serving

1 apple (Jonathan, Jonagold, Rome or Granny Smith)
2 tsp. brown sugar
½ tsp. ground cinnamon
1 tsp. butter
5 to 6 raisins, optional

Directions

Cut 1 piece of heavy-duty foil large enough to wrap around
the apple. Cut the core out of the apple and remove it. Cut
1″ off the bottom of the core to use as a plug. Discard the
top portion of core. Insert the plug back in the bottom of the
apple and set it on the foil. In a small bowl, mix the brown
sugar and cinnamon. Fill the core space in the apple with
2 alternating layers of butter and the brown sugar mixture.
Add raisins, if desired. Wrap the stuffed apple snugly in foil,
sealing it well.

Cooking Methods

 Preheat oven to 375°. Place foil-wrapped apple on center rack and bake for 30 to 40 minutes or until apple is soft. Let apple cool a few minutes before opening foil.

 Wrap apple in a second layer of foil. Place foil-wrapped apple on medium-hot embers for 20 to 30 minutes or until apple is soft. Let apple cool a few minutes before opening foil.

 Preheat grill to medium heat. Place foil-wrapped apple on the grill over direct heat, close lid and cook for 25 to 30 minutes or until apple is soft. Let apple cool a few minutes before opening foil.

Variations

• Instead of using 1 whole apple, cut the apple into chunks. In a small bowl, mix 1 teaspoon sugar, 1 tablespoon biscuit baking mix and a pinch of cinnamon. Stir apple chunks into the mixture. Spoon mixture onto sprayed foil and wrap foil around apples in a tent pack. Cook as directed using lower heat and a shorter cooking time.

• Stuff the apple with caramel candies and a dab of butter

• Stuff the apple with chopped pecans, dates and shredded coconut and top with brown sugar.

Sweet Banana Boat

Makes 1 serving

1 firm banana
1 T. miniature milk chocolate chips
2 T. miniature marshmallows

Directions

Peel back 1 long strip of banana peel from the inside of the curve but leave the bottom end attached. With a spoon, scoop out some of the exposed flesh of banana as if making a boat. Fill opening in banana with chocolate chips and marshmallows, pressing them down lightly. Replace the strip of banana peel. Cut 1 piece of foil large enough to wrap around the stuffed banana. Wrap banana tightly in foil. After cooking as directed, carefully unwrap foil, peel skin back and eat dessert with a spoon.

Cooking Methods

 Preheat oven to 350°. Place foil-wrapped banana on a baking sheet and bake for 10 to 15 minutes or until filling is melted.

 Place foil-wrapped banana on warm embers and cook for 5 to 15 minutes or until filling is melted.

 Preheat grill to medium heat. Set foil-wrapped banana on the grill over direct heat, close lid and cook for 5 to 15 minutes or until filling is melted.

Variations

- Substitute chocolate-covered raisins for the chocolate chips or add plain raisins with the other ingredients.

- Break up a chocolate bar with almonds and use it in place of the chocolate chips.

- Omit the marshmallows. Spread 2 teaspoons peanut butter into the banana followed by chocolate chips.

- Try using dark or semi-sweet chocolate chips.

- For a banana split treat, fill banana with small amounts of chocolate chips, marshmallows, pineapple preserves, chopped nuts and small pieces of maraschino cherries.

S'more Burritos Please!

Makes 1 serving

1 (8″) flour tortilla
2 to 3 T. crunchy peanut butter
3 T. miniature marshmallows
3 T. miniature chocolate chips

Directions

Cut 1 piece of foil about 12″ long. Set tortilla on the center of the foil. Spread the peanut butter over the tortilla, almost to the edges. Sprinkle the marshmallows and chocolate chips over half of the peanut butter. Fold in the sides and then roll up the tortilla like a burrito, beginning with the chocolate chip side. Wrap foil around burrito in a flat pack.

Cooking Methods

 Preheat oven to 375°. Set foil-wrapped burrito on a baking sheet and bake for 8 to 12 minutes or until tortilla is warm and chocolate is melted.

 Place double-wrapped burrito on warm embers and cook for 5 to 15 minutes or until tortilla is warm and chocolate is melted. Move as needed to obtain even heating.

 Preheat grill to medium-low heat. Place foil-wrapped burrito on the grill over direct heat, close lid and cook for 5 to 10 minutes or until tortilla is warm and chocolate is melted.

Variations

• Omit the peanut butter and marshmallows. On the center of the tortilla, sprinkle the chocolate chips and ¼ cup fresh raspberries. After rolling it up burrito-style, brush the outside with melted margarine and wrap in foil. After cooking, brush with more melted butter and sprinkle with powdered sugar.

• Serve burrito warm with a scoop of vanilla ice cream.

115

Pineapple Upside-Down Cake

Makes 6 servings

6 pineapple rings
6 cake donuts
6 T. soft margarine, divided
6 T. brown sugar, divided

Directions

Drain pineapple, reserving the liquid. Cut 6 pieces of foil, each large enough to wrap around 1 donut. Set 1 donut on each piece of foil. Spread 1 tablespoon margarine on top of each donut. Sprinkle 1 tablespoon brown sugar on top of margarine. Top each donut with 1 pineapple ring. Drizzle 1 to 2 teaspoons of reserved pineapple juice in center of each donut. Wrap foil snugly around each serving in a flat pack.

Cooking Methods

 Preheat oven to 350°. Place foil packs in a 9 x 13˝ baking dish and bake for 12 to 20 minutes or until pineapple is warm and brown sugar is syrupy.

 Place double-wrapped foil packs on warm embers and cook for 8 to 15 minutes, moving as needed. Cook until pineapple is warm and brown sugar is syrupy.

 Preheat grill to medium-low heat. Place foil packs on the grill over direct heat, close lid and cook for 8 to 15 minutes or until pineapple is warm and brown sugar is syrupy.

Variations

• Use 6 slices of purchased pound cake in place of the donuts.

• Place 1 whole maraschino cherry in the center of each pineapple ring.

• Use round sponge cake dessert cups in place of the donuts.

Gingerbread Cake in an Orange Shell

Makes 12 servings

1 (14.5 oz.) pkg. gingerbread cake mix (with egg and water)
12 thick-skinned oranges
Caramel ice cream topping

Directions

Roll the oranges on a hard surface to soften the membranes inside. Cut the top fourth off each orange. Use a sharp knife to separate the pulp from the white membranes of each shell. With a spoon, carefully remove all the orange pulp without tearing the peel. Eat fruit or set it aside for later use. Prepare the cake mix as directed on package. Spoon batter into hollowed orange shells, filling each one about ⅔ full. Cut 1 (10˝) piece of heavy-duty foil for each orange shell. Set orange in center of foil. Wrap foil up and around sides of shell, leaving the top open. Crimp foil around the top of shell and flatten bottom so orange stands upright. After baking, poke several fork holes in the top of each cake and drizzle with caramel ice cream topping. Eat warm with a spoon right from the orange shell.

Cooking Methods

 Preheat oven to 400°. Place foil-wrapped oranges in a 9 x 13″ baking dish and bake for 30 to 40 minutes or until a toothpick inserted in cake comes out clean.

 Place foil-wrapped oranges on hot coals for 15 to 25 minutes or until a toothpick inserted in cake comes out clean. Move them as needed for even baking.

 Preheat grill to high heat. Place foil-wrapped oranges on the grill over indirect heat, close lid and bake for 15 to 25 minutes or until toothpick inserted in cake comes out clean.

Variations

• Try a chocolate, yellow or spice cake mix in place of the gingerbread mix.

• Make part of the gingerbread batter in the orange shells and bake any remaining batter like traditional muffins in an oven, using paper or foil liner cups in a muffin pan.

FYI – Cooking in an orange peel may not save any time but, it is fun to do and easy to clean up if you are camping!

Apple Crisp

Makes 4 to 6 servings

4 C. thinly sliced apples
1 C. sugar
1 tsp. ground cinnamon
¾ C. rolled oats
¼ C. butter, melted
¼ C. brown sugar
Whipped topping or vanilla ice cream, optional

Directions

Cut 2 (14˝) pieces of heavy-duty foil and stack them together.
Place an 8˝ round baking pan upside down. Wrap both sheets
of foil over the bottom of the pan, crimping foil like pan
edges to make a sturdy pan shape. Remove baking pan. Spray
inside of foil pan with nonstick vegetable spray. In a medium
bowl, mix the sliced apples, sugar and cinnamon. Spread
apple mixture in foil pan. In a clean bowl, combine oats,
melted butter and brown sugar until crumbly. Spread mixture
over apples. Cook as directed. Serve warm with whipped
topping or vanilla ice cream, if desired.

Cooking Methods

Preheat oven to 350°. Set foil baking pan on a baking sheet and bake for 28 to 35 minutes or until apples are tender and mixture is bubbly.

Place a grill over hot coals. Set the foil baking pan on the grill and cook for 18 to 25 minutes or until apples are tender. Move pan as needed to obtain even heating.

Preheat grill to medium heat. Set the foil baking pan on the grill over indirect heat, close lid and cook for 18 to 25 minutes or until apples are tender. Move pan as needed to obtain even heating.

Variations

• Add ¼ cup raisins, dried cherries or dried cranberries to apple mixture. Let mixture stand for 10 minutes to soften the dried fruit before putting the dessert together.

• Use fresh peaches in place of the apples.

• Use canned apple or peach pie filling in place of the fresh apples and sugar. Make crumble topping as directed. Shorten cooking time slightly. Fruit should be hot and bubbly.

Candied Banana Slices

Makes 4 servings

4 large ripe bananas
¼ C. dark brown sugar
3 T. apricot jam
2 T. butter, melted
2 T. lemon juice
¼ C. dry sherry

Directions

Peel the bananas and cut them into 1″ slices. Cut 1 piece of
heavy-duty foil large enough to wrap around all the banana
slices. Spray foil with nonstick vegetable spray and arrange
the bananas on foil. Crimp foil edges enough to hold in
liquids. In a small bowl, combine the brown sugar, apricot
jam, melted butter, lemon juice and sherry. Spread mixture
evenly over banana slices. Wrap foil around banana slices in
a tent pack.

Cooking Methods

Preheat oven to 350°. Place foil pack on a baking sheet and bake for 15 minutes. Carefully cut top of foil pack open. Bake an additional 15 minutes.

Place double-wrapped foil pack on warm embers for 10 to 15 minutes or until warmed. Carefully cut top of foil pack open and cook for a few more minutes.

Preheat grill to medium heat. Place foil pack on the grill over direct heat, close lid and cook for 8 to 12 minutes. Carefully cut top of foil pack open. Bake an additional 10 minutes, moving to indirect heat as needed.

Variation

• Substitute peach jam for the apricot jam and peach or vanilla flavored coffee syrup for the sherry.

Peachy Mallow

Makes 1 serving

1 peach
1 tsp. butter
2 tsp. brown sugar
1 marshmallow
Ground cinnamon

Directions

Cut the peach in half. Remove and discard the pit. Cut
1 piece of heavy-duty foil large enough to wrap around the
whole peach. Spray foil with nonstick vegetable spray. Set
1 peach half on the foil, cut side up. Place butter in the hollow
of the peach. Sprinkle brown sugar on the cut area of peach.
Set 1 marshmallow in the peach hollow and sprinkle with
cinnamon. Place the other peach half on top, with cut sides
together. Wrap foil snugly around peach, sealing it well.

Cooking Methods

 Preheat oven to 350°. Place foil-wrapped peach on a baking sheet and bake for 8 to 15 minutes or until peach is warm and marshmallow is soft.

 Place foil-wrapped peach on warm embers for 5 to 10 minutes or until peach is warm and marshmallow is soft. Move pack as needed to obtain even heating.

 Preheat grill to medium heat. Place foil-wrapped peach on the grill over direct heat, close lid and cook for 5 to 10 minutes or until peach is warm and marshmallow is soft.

Variations

• Use canned, sliced peaches in place of the fresh peach. Spray 1 large piece of foil with nonstick vegetable spray. Place half of the drained sliced peaches on foil and sprinkle with butter pieces and brown sugar. Place some miniature marshmallows on top and cover with another layer of sliced peaches. Wrap foil around peaches in a tent pack and cook as directed.

• For a softer peach texture, increase cooking time.

Index

Foil Facts & Cooking Tips

Breakfasts

Main Dishes

Index

Potatoes & Other Vegetables

Sandwiches

Desserts

Notes & Ideas For Foil Cooking